ARE DEMONS THE CAUSE OF YOUR SICKNESS?

(REVISED EDITION)

Author: Dr. Ebenezer N. Caternor

Copyright © 2010 by DR. EBENEZER N. CATERNOR

ARE DEMONS THE CAUSE OF YOUR SICKNESS?
(REVISED EDITION)
by DR. EBENEZER N. CATERNOR

Printed in the United States of America

ISBN 9781615798810

All rights reserved solely by the author. The author guarantees all contents are original and do not infringe upon the legal rights of any other person or work. No part of this book may be reproduced in any form without the permission of the author. The views expressed in this book are not necessarily those of the publisher.

Unless otherwise indicated, Bible quotations are taken from NKJV of the Bible. Copyright © 1990 by Thomas Nelson, Inc.

www.xulonpress.com

DEDICATION

This book is dedicated to the Congregation of the Miracle Temple Assembly of God, Silver Spring, Maryland, U.S.A.

As the Pastor, the Holy Spirit used and continue to use this Congregation as the battle field to teach me many of the things I now know about the Devil, demons and their *modus operandi.* The knowledge I have acquired has benefited me immensely in my *Healing and Deliverance* Ministry. I give all the glory and honor to Jesus Christ, my Lord and my Savior.

FOREWORD

I have been in the *Healing & Deliverance Ministry* in full time for the past twelve years. Although there are a number of books out there on this subject, written by great servants of God; I decided to write this book to re-emphasize the controversial fact that the Devil and demons are the cause of many human sicknesses and diseases. When demons are the cause of any disease, sickness, illness or pain in the human body, Medical Science and Pharmacology may not be able to help.

This book is meant to draw my readers' attention to seek pastoral spiritual help if Medical Science and Pharmacology have no clues to their ailments. I believe if everyone knows this basic truth, they will seek help from the right place when they need it. These patients must seek help from Pastors in the Healing and Deliverance Ministry where Jesus Christ is the center of it all.

Can Christians have demons indwelling them? Theologians have debated this topic for several decades which has created a dichotomy among them. I have tried to look at this controversial topic from another perspective. This is an aspect of my book I present to theologians who have an interest in this topic to take a look and their comments are most welcome.

Most pastors from Africa know and talk about "Spiritual marriage" but I did not find any printed material on this subject. I have defined what I know to be "Spiritual marriage." I have also discussed the consequences of a "Spiritual marriage" and given some details on how to break such a marriage to set the victims free. The consequences of a "Spiritual marriage" are numerous and unknown to many people. I have also discussed the consequences of generational curses and covenants although I am aware that some people do not believe in the effect of such curses.

I want to thank all the great men and women of God whose books/articles (listed in the End Notes) I consulted as I wrote this book. I wish to express my sincere thanks and appreciation to Ms Lucian Hammond for presenting to me the book *Everything You Need To Know To Write, Publish, & Market Your Book* by Patrika Vaughn. This book was useful to me throughout the period of writing.

Once again I wish to extend my sincere gratitude to Ms Lucian Hammond for all her encouraging words throughout the period. It is my sincere prayer that everyone who reads this book will find something useful in it. We give the glory to Jesus Christ.

Dr. Ebenezer N. Caternor

MEDICAL SCIENCE, PHARMACOLOGY AND MEDICAL DOCTORS

I wish to state clearly that I have great respect for Medical Doctors, Pharmacologists and all other paramedical staff for the wonderful work they perform to save human lives daily. All I am saying in this book is that when a particular sickness, disease, illness or pain goes beyond their wisdom and medical knowledge; and pharmacology does not bring relief either, then it is most likely that demons may be the cause. In such a situation it is only spiritual deliverance in the name of Jesus Christ that can bring healing. Such patients should seek help from an anointed Pastor of God in the Healing and Deliverance Ministry where Jesus Christ is Lord and Savior. God bless all of you.

Dr. Ebenezer N. Caternor

TABLE OF CONTENTS

Foreword vii

Introduction
The Prevalence of Human Illness xvii
Definition of Human Health xviii
Definitions xix
The Objective of this Book xxi
Limitation xxii

Chapter One
The Devil—Preamble 23
The Origin of the Devil...24
The Omniscience of God 28

Chapter Two
The Origin of Demons...30
How many Angels (demons)
   were cast down to the Earth? 33

Chapter Three
Present Habitation of Satan and Demons 35
Demons and the Human Body 38

Chapter Four
The Kingdom of Satan and Hierarchy 39
The Boundaries of Satan's Kingdom 40
Satan's Army 40
The High Command Structure of Satan 41

Chapter Five
The Nature of Demons 43
Demons and Physical Bodies 43
Marks of Personality of Demons 45
Character Traits of Demons 46
Capabilities of Demons 48
Demons Speak in the First Person Singular 49

Chapter Six
Demons in the Old and New Testaments 52

Chapter Seven
The Origin of Human Illness 56
Other Causes of Human Illness 57

Chapter Eight
Are Demons the Cause of Every Sickness? 61
When are Demons the Cause of a Sickness? 62

Chapter Nine
Strange Causes of Illnesses 66

Chapter Ten
Role of Demons in Illness 70
Duties of Individual Demons 72
Demons that cause Severe Pain in the Human body 75

Chapter Eleven
Mental Illness 77
Schizophrenia is definitely demonic 80

Chapter Twelve
Why do Demons Love to Inhabit Humans? 82
How do Demons Inhabit Humans? 83
Demons in Little Children 84
Why not cast the Demon Out? 86

Chapter Thirteen
Is it Demon Possession or Demonization? 88

Chapter Fourteen
Physical Manifestations of Demons 91
Do all Demons Manifest? 94
Demons that use Deception to Evade Expulsion 95

Chapter Fifteen
Can Demons Indwell Christians? 97
Demonization and Demonic Interference 101
Demons Can Interfere in the Normal Functioning
    of the Human Body 103
It was an "Issue of Blood" 104
Medical Science, Pharmacology and Medical Doctors ... 106

Chapter Sixteen
Spiritual Marriage 107
A Gentleman who could not marry 108
Demon Interference with Pregnancy 109
Successive Miscarriages may be a sign of a
    Spiritual Marriage 110
Breaking a Spiritual Marriage 111

Chapter Seventeen
Covenants/Agreements with the Devil and
 Demonic Shrines/Altars 114
Generational Curses and Covenants.................................116
Consequences of Generational Curses and
 Demonic Covenants..116
Seek Help as Quickly as Possible 119
So what have I Been Trying to Convey to You?................120
Our Immutable Confesssion 121

Notes **123**

INTRODUCTION

The Prevalence of Human Illness

The sin of Adam and Eve brought instant spiritual death to them. Their sin was the disobedience of God's command: "And the Lord God commanded the man, saying, 'of every tree of the garden you may freely eat; but of the tree of the knowledge of good and evil you shall not eat, for in the day that you eat of it you shall surely die'" (Genesis 2:16-17). The same sin brought spiritual death to the entire human race and also face to face with disease, sickness, illness, pain and eventual physical death. Consequently, humanity needs no introduction to disease, sickness, illness and pain because mankind lives with the problem on daily basis.

Although all humans are susceptible to disease and sickness, the underdeveloped areas of the world (Africa, Asia, India, etc.) experience poorer health which is attributed to poor unhygienic living conditions. Throughout the past centuries, man has found some explanations and cures for a large number of diseases, sicknesses, and illnesses through medical science and pharmacology. However, there are certain illnesses which mankind has neither found explanations nor cures.

Definition of Human Health

The magnitude of the problem of poor health among the populations of the world saw the formation of the World Health Organization (WHO) after the Second World War. In order to measure improvement in the quality of health among the populations of the world, it became necessary to define human health. The WHO defines human health as "the mode of being healthy, to include a state of complete physical, mental and social well-being and not merely the absence of disease or infirmity" (WHO, 1946). When these conditions are not fulfilled, then one can be considered to have an illness or be ill.[1]

The Christian Medical Commission (CMC) of the World Council of Churches (WCC) also defines human health as follows: "Health is a dynamic state of well-being of the individual and the society; of physical, mental, spiritual, economic, political and social well-being; of being in harmony with each other, with the material environment and with God.[2]

Definitions

Physical Illness. The *Freedictionary Encyclopedia* defines physical illness as: "Any abnormal condition of the physical body or mind that causes discomfort, dysfunction, or distress to the person afflicted. Sometimes physical illness is used broadly to include injuries, disabilities, infections, symptoms, deviant behaviors, and typical variations of structure and function. Food-borne illness or food poisoning is any illness resulting from the consumption of food contaminated with bacteria, toxins, viruses, or parasites."[3]

Spiritual Illness. An illness that has no natural cause or explanation may be described as "spiritual." It means that demons may be the cause of such an illness. Medical science and pharmacology may not be able to help when the disease is spiritual. The only remedy is through spiritual deliverance in the name of Jesus Christ.

Mental Illness. The *Freedictionary Encyclopedia* defines "Mental Illness" as follows: "Mental Illness (or emotional disability, cognitive dysfunction) is a broad generic label for a category of illnesses that may include affective or emotional instability, behavioral deregulation, and/or cognitive dysfunction or impairment." Specific illnesses known as mental illnesses include major depression, generalized anxiety disorder, schizophrenia, and attention deficit hyperactivity disorder.[4]

Sickness is defined as a particular disease or malady. The state or an instance of being sick; illness.[5]

Disease is defined as a disordered or abnormal condition of an organ or other part of an organism resulting from the effect of genetic or developmental errors, infection, nutritional deficiency, toxicity, or unfavorable environmental factors; illness; sickness.[6]

Illness is defined as an unhealthy condition, poor health; indisposition; sickness.[7] It is a subjective state in a human, marked by feelings of deviation from the normal healthy state; a term not thought to be applicable to animals.[8] It could be inferred from the definitions above that a *disease* could make a human being either *sick* or *ill*. Consequently, in this book, illness, sickness and disease shall be used interchangeably.

Demons/unclean spirits/evil spirits. Demons are the fallen angels associated with Satan in his rebellion against God. The Holy Scriptures speak of angels that are aligned with the Devil. In the famous passage about the kingdom of heaven in Matthew 25:31-46, Jesus spoke of the "everlasting fire, prepared for the devil and his angels" (v.41). Jesus gave his disciples power over unclean spirits to cast them out (Matthew 10:1). In Acts 19:12, Paul used handkerchiefs, anointed in the power of the Holy Spirit, to drive out evil spirits from people. It could be inferred from the foregoing that Scripture refers to demons as unclean spirits or evil spirits. Therefore demons, unclean spirits and evil spirits are synonymous terms.

The Objective of this Book

It is an open secret that Medical science and Pharmacology have found cures for many illnesses that afflict humanity. However, there are certain illnesses for which no cures have been found yet. This book will attempt to show that demons sometimes play a role in causing human illnesses. When demons are involved, medical science and pharmacology have no answers—the only cure is through deliverance when we cast out the demons in the name of Jesus Christ. Therefore, the objective of this book is to draw readers' attention to the fact that there are sicknesses which are caused by demons. Therefore, when medical science and pharmacology fail to find a cure for your sickness, disease or pain, please seek help from any Pastor in the healing and deliverance ministry where Jesus Christ is Lord and Savior.

Limitation

This book is limited to human illnesses only as follows: Any illness that affects the proper healthy functioning of the human body; any human behavior that may be looked upon by the larger or majority of the human community as abnormal; anything that causes pain or discomfort to the human body, whether seen or unseen, both in the physical and spiritual realms.

CHAPTER ONE

THE DEVIL
Preamble

"The wind blows where it wishes, and you hear the sound of it, but cannot tell where it comes from and where it goes..."(John 3:8). Truly, we do not see the wind, per se, but when it blows, we see its effect on the environment. Almost all cultures of all the nations of the world agree that there is a spiritual realm in addition to the physical realm in which we live.

Humans see all the activities that take place in the physical realm and quickly acknowledge them. However, because we do not see into the spiritual realm, we do not easily acknowledge the activities that go on there. Like the wind, which we cannot see except its effect on the environment, so also are the activities of the spiritual realm which we cannot see but may seriously affect our physical realm, especially humans and human activities.

I am aware that the topic for this book delves into a very controversial arena because the arguments to be advanced are based on activities in the spiritual realm which humans do not normally see. You may be surprised to learn that some of the activities in the spiritual realm by demons may cause certain illnesses in humans. At this juncture, it is pertinent to trace the origin of the Devil, the leader of the demons.

The Origin of the Devil

There are two major mistakes which the human race makes concerning the Devil and demons. One is to disbelieve in their existence as most people do. This is a natural reaction because most people do not see these devils. The other mistake is that some people believe that the devils exist but show virtually no interest in them; in other words they try to ignore them. I am not sure which group you belong but I want you to know that the Devil and demons exist and you should know how to deal with them.

Who is the Devil and what is his origin? The Devil, also known as Lucifer and Satan was first mentioned in the Scriptures in Genesis 3:1 and was referred to as *the serpent*.

He was created as an angel. Speaking of Jesus Christ, Colossians 1:16 says: "For by Him all things were created that are in heaven and that are on earth, visible and invisible...." Since this Scripture presupposes that God created all things (Genesis 1 and 2), it could be inferred that Lucifer is a created *being*.

Indeed the Devil was one of God's creatures who being filled with pride, rebelled and lost his position in heaven. Lucifer later set up his own kingdom in hatred against God. I personally believe that originally, God prepared hell and the Lake of Fire for Satan and his demons only (Matthew 25:41). However, the Devil probably swore that he will not spend eternity in the Lake of Fire alone. Therefore he is doing everything possible to deceive humans so he [Devil] could get as many human souls as possible to spend eternity with him in the Lake of Fire.

It could be inferred from the foregoing that the Devil, Satan and Lucifer refer to one and the same personality. When was Lucifer created? Because there is no mention of the creation of angels in the "creation story" of Genesis 1 and 2, it may be presumed that all the angels including Lucifer were created prior to the story beginning from Genesis 1:1.

Archangels

It is generally assumed among Christians that there are three archangels. It is also generally believed in Christendom that Michael was the archangel in charge of all the military matters of God—the fighting angel (Revelation 12:7). The angel Gabriel was the communication angel who carried messages to God's people (Luke 1:26-33). Finally, Lucifer is said to be the leader of the choir in praise and worship of the living God in heaven.

Contrary to this popular belief that there are three archangels, only Michael is referred to in Scripture as an archangel (Jude 9). The other two (Gabriel and Lucifer) are not clearly referred to in the Scriptures as archangels. Even the assertion that Lucifer was the archangel in charge of the host of angels who worship in heaven has no clear Scriptural support.

Lucifer the Angel who became the Devil and Satan

Certainly, God did not create Lucifer as the Devil. We also know that God who is perfect in his holiness never created anything sinful and the fact that he did not create the Devil as he is now. So when did Lucifer supposed to be in charge of the heavenly choir, become the Devil? Certainly, Satan was a high-ranking angel who rebelled in heaven and became the enemy of God and all that is holy, right, and godly.

It is clear that Isaiah 14:4-21 and Ezekiel 28:12-19 speak of the Kings of Babylon and Tyre respectively; however a closer look at these Scriptures reveals that these passages seem to describe what happened in heaven just before Lucifer lost his position. In the book of Ezekiel, it is said, presumably of Satan, "...you were the seal of perfection, full of wisdom and perfect in beauty...from the day you were created, till iniquity was found in you (Ezekiel 28:12, 15). In the Isaiah passage, Lucifer said "I will ascend into heaven, I will exalt my throne above the stars of God; I will also sit on the mount of the congregation....I will be like the Most High" (Isaiah 14:13-14).

From the preceding paragraph, it could be inferred that Satan conceived a thought of rebellion out of pride to overthrow God. In modern military parlance, one may say Lucifer planned a coup d`etat which was abortive. How long did Lucifer take to plan the abortive coup d`etat? The Scriptures are silent on how long it took Lucifer to plan his rebellion. Probably, it took him several days, several weeks, several months, or a number of years.

Lucifer, who probably had authority over a large number of angels succeeded in deceiving some of those under him, most probably from the heavenly choir, to withdraw their loyalty to God. Subsequently, Lucifer led his "loyalists" in a rebellion against God. Isaiah 14:15 says: "Yet you shall be brought down to Sheol, to the lowest depths of the Pit." Therefore, in a ruthless response to the uprising, God cast Lucifer and his dissident angels from his presence in heaven. This view of Lucifer's fall, to become the Devil, is also supported by Revelation 12:7-9:

> And war broke out in heaven: Michael and his angels fought against the dragon [Lucifer]; and the dragon [Lucifer] and his angels fought, but they [Lucifer and his angels] did not prevail, nor was a place found for them[Lucifer and his angels] in heaven any longer. So the great dragon [Lucifer] was cast out, that serpent of old, called the Devil and Satan, who deceives the whole world; he [Lucifer] was cast to the earth, and his[Lucifer] angels were cast out with him.

The Omniscience of God

The Scriptures declare the omniscience of God in Isaiah 40:14 "With whom did He take counsel, and who instructed Him,...who taught Him knowledge, and showed Him the way of understanding." Also in Colossians 2:2-3, it says "...to the knowledge of the mystery of God, both of the Father and of Christ, in whom are hidden all the treasures of wisdom and knowledge." Therefore, it may be presumed that there is nothing hidden from God by way of knowledge, in other words He is omniscient. Consequently, someone may ask a pertinent question. Didn't God know about the plan and rebellion of Lucifer? It may be presumed here that God knew about the plan and activities of Lucifer but allowed him to pursue his selfish *will*. Indeed, God never interferes in the *free will* that he has given to the angels and to humans.

CHAPTER TWO

The Origin of Demons

From the previous chapter on the origin of the Devil, it was shown that the Devil rebelled with a large number of angels. These rebellious angels who willfully decided to follow Satan in his abortive coup d`etat were all expelled from heaven. So who are the demons and where did they come from? It is certain that Lucifer did not possess the capability to create any *beings* because he was a created *being* himself. Consequently, it could be inferred that any other creatures working with Lucifer must be the angels who were expelled with him. Therefore the angels who fell with Lucifer must be the demons in the world today.

Included in the Faith of the Early Fathers is their belief that the Devil was an angel who persuaded many angels in a rebellion against God; and how they were expelled from heaven. In the third century, Origen (ca. 185-254), a theologian from Alexandria wrote on the origin of the Devil and demons. He wrote to confirm the faith of the Early Fathers in the existence of the Devil and demons and how they were expelled from heaven.[1]

Does Scripture support Origen's assertions? Absolutely, there are a number of Scripture verses that describe the origin and current condition of demons: (1) "for if God did not spare the angels who sinned, but cast them down to hell and delivered them into chains of darkness, to be reserved for judgment" (2 Peter 2:4); (2) "and the angels who did not keep their proper domain, but left their own habitation, He has reserved in everlasting chains under darkness for the judgment of the great day" (Jude 6); and (3) Revelation 12:7-9 (quoted in the previous chapter).

I support the popular view that the angels who were expelled from heaven with Lucifer became the demons. This suggestion that the angels who fell away with Lucifer became demons is also supported by a number of theologians. Sumrall supports the view that the angels who fell with Lucifer became the demons, or evil spirits in the world.[2] The United Church of God also supports the view that "the rebellious angels are demons and that they are fallen angels ... reduced to hatred and bitterness toward God and His holy purpose for humanity."[3]

On the origin of demons, there are three separate theories that are usually mentioned: (1) they are the disembodied spirits of a pre-Adamic race, destroyed by God (this idea seems to fit the "gap theory" of creation); (2) they are the "Nephilim" of Genesis 6, the disembodied spirits of a mutant race created by the mating of angels and humans; (3) they are the original angelic creation that fell with Lucifer. I strongly support the view that the fallen angels became demons and close associates of the Devil. They are together referred to as "...the rulers of the darkness of this age..." (Ephesians 6:12).

I do not support the assertion that demons had their origin in a pre-Adamite age because there is no clear Scriptural evidence to support this belief. Among the many sources consulted for this book, very few theologians believe in this theory on the origin of demons. A close study of Genesis 6 does not also reveal the suggestion that demons are the "Nephilim," neither does it clearly say that the "sons of God" are angelic beings.

Although the origin of demons is not clearly stated in the Scriptures, it is reasonable to infer that the fallen angels became the demons. The preceding inference is in consonance with the fact that Lucifer has no power to create any *beings* which leads to the reasonable conclusion that the fallen angels expelled with him became the demons who are working with him. I tentatively support the view that demons are the angels who joined Lucifer to fight the war in heaven and were subsequently cast down to the earth by the God who created all things, visible and invincible. This probably leads us to our next question.

How many Angels (demons) were cast down to the Earth?

How many fallen angels were expelled from heaven with Lucifer? A number of arguments have been advanced by theologians in support of their suggestions. Many of these theologians base their explanations on Revelation 12:4 which states "his tail drew a third of the stars of heaven and threw them to the earth...." Assuming this interpretation is correct, and since the angels are without number, "ten thousand times ten thousand, and thousands of thousands" (Revelation 5:11); the number of Satan's angels (demons) may be beyond human imagination.

Charles Kraft, however, does not support theologians who interpret Revelation 12:4 as indicating that one-third of the angels in heaven sided with Satan.[4] I support Kraft on this issue because there is nothing specific in Revelation 12:4 to indicate that one-third of the stars represent one-third of the angels. I will interpret "his tail drew a third of the stars of heaven and threw them to the earth" to imply a degree of compulsion or coercion—he threw them to the earth. However, all the activities of Lucifer's rebellion indicate that he convinced the angels who sided with him; and subsequently, they willingly followed him. This argument does not support the assertion that the "stars" in Revelation 12:4 were angels who were forcefully thrown down to the earth by Lucifer. Rather, the angels together with Satan who rebelled were expelled from heaven by God.

In the light of the foregoing paragraphs, it may be inferred that Scripture has neither indicated the exact total number of angels in heaven nor the exact number that was expelled with Lucifer. We may however conclude that a large number, probably thousands of thousands or millions of angels were expelled from heaven.

CHAPTER THREE

Present Habitation of Satin and Demons

Where did Satan and his rebellious fallen angels go when God banished them from his presence in heaven? There is no passage in Scripture that describes any specific location to which Lucifer and his fallen angels were banished. However, putting a number of Scripture passages together may help to identify a possible location.

2 Corinthians 12:2 declares: "I know a man in Christ who fourteen years ago—whether in the body I do not know, or whether out of the body I do not know, God knows—such a one was caught up to the *third heaven*." Revelation 8:13 states: "And I looked, and I heard an angel flying through the *midst of heaven*...." Revelation 19:17 also states: "Then I saw an angel standing in the sun; and he cried with a

loud voice, saying to all the birds that fly in the *midst of heaven*...." Then 2 Chronicles 2:6 says: "But who is able to build Him a temple, since heaven and the *heaven of heavens* cannot contain Him?....." These passages identify at least two different heavens: a middle heaven and a third heaven or the *heaven of heavens*.

From the preceding paragraphs, we may identify three different areas as "heaven" in Scripture. First, the *visible heaven* above the earth where we see birds fly. Second, is the *mid-heaven* which is described in Revelation 8:13, finally, the *third heaven* which is the highest of all and is the sacred place that King Solomon refers to in 2 Chronicles 2:6, as the *Heaven of heavens*.

Indeed, there are three heavens. I believe that the earth, including the stratosphere, is the *first heaven*. The *second heaven* is where Satan has established his throne, and there he reigns as "the prince of the power of the air" (Ephesians 2:2). God's throne is established in the *third heaven* also referred to as the Heaven *of heavens* (2 Chronicles 2:6; 2 Corinthians 12: 2).

God is omnipresent and therefore someone might ask whether God is present also in the second heaven where Satan is believed to have established his seat of government? Although God is omnipresent, he does not reveal himself everywhere—only at the places he wants to reveal himself. I am of the view that God will not reveal himself in the presence of Satan or in hell except for some special reason. Isaiah 43:2 says "when you pass through the waters, I will be with you; and through the rivers, they shall not overflow you...." God is certainly present everywhere at the same time, but he reveals himself when and where he wants to do so. Jeremiah 23:23-24 supports the preceding statements as follows: "Am I a God near at hand" says the Lord, "and not a God afar off? Can anyone hide himself in secret places, so I shall not see him?" says the Lord; "Do I not fill heaven and earth?" says the Lord. God is certainly omnipresent but he does not reveal himself everywhere all the time.

Satan and his rebellious angels (now demons) were thrown out of heaven as disembodied spirits and they are here on the earth. It appears that although Satan has established his throne in the *second heaven,* call it his operational headquarters, his area of operation and influence is on the earth among humans where his host of demons are ceaselessly active doing his bidding. Demons virtually live wherever humans live because the latter are his targets to attack and destroy.

Demons and the Human Body

Demons love to dwell in human bodies in order to express themselves in the physical realm. Therefore the human body can be a habitation for demons if given the opportunity. This assertion is supported by the fact that on numerous occasions, Jesus cast out spirits of deafness and dumbness from people (Mark 9:25). He also cast out spirits of *infirmity* (weakness) (Luke 13:11). Therefore, it is reasonable to infer that an evil spirit may dwell in the human body if given the opportunity, and may not depart until someone casts it out with divine authority in the name of Jesus Christ. Based on these Scriptures, I know for sure that demons may dwell in humans. The Gadarene demoniac described in Mark 5:1-18 is a Scriptural support for the assertion that demons may inhabit human bodies if given the opportunity. We will look at how demons may enter and inhabit human bodies later in this book.

CHAPTER FOUR

The Kingdom of Satan and Hierarchy

Has Satan established a kingdom? Luke 11:17-18 states: "But He, knowing their thoughts, said to them: 'Every kingdom divided against itself is brought to desolation, and a house divided against a house falls. If Satan also is divided against himself, how will his kingdom stand? Because you say I cast out demons by Beelzebub.'" In this Scripture passage, Jesus Christ shows clearly that Satan has a kingdom; and in Ephesians 6:12, Paul shows the hierarchy of Satan's kingdom: "For we do not wrestle against flesh and blood, but against principalities, against powers, against the rulers of the darkness of this age, against spiritual hosts of wickedness in the heavenly places."

The Boundaries of Satan's Kingdom

When Lucifer was cast out of heaven, he did not stop his rebellion but went ahead to set up his own kingdom in opposition to God's kingdom. Every kingdom has a seat of government and has boundaries. Where is the seat of Satan's kingdom and where are its boundaries? It was asserted earlier that Satan's throne is in the second heaven from where he directs all activities in his kingdom. Satan's area of influence certainly includes the second heaven, where his throne is established; and the first heaven including the Earth. Obviously, wherever there are human beings, Satan's kingdom extends to that place because humans are his main targets for destruction.

Satan's Army

Satan and his cohorts fought a war in heaven in their rebellion against God; therefore, it may be reasonable to infer that they are organized like an army to fight. Like human armies in the physical realm with various levels of command, it has been asserted that Satan's host of demons may be organized on similar lines. George Birch supports the assertion that Satan's kingdom is well organized as described in Ephesians 6:12.[1] Steve Gallagher also supports the assertion that Satan has probably organized his forces into an army.[2] I believe that there is a well organized army of demons who operate under the directives of the Devil himself.

The High Command Structure of Satan

Do all the demons belong to the four main groups mentioned in Ephesians 6:12? If Satan has probably organized his fighting forces similar to what exists in the army in the physical realm, then the levels in the hierarchy may be more than the four mentioned in Ephesians 6:12. If this assumption is true, then the four levels mentioned, may refer to only the "top command level structure." I believe there may be several levels below the top command level to control the thousands of thousands or millions of demons involved. All the spiritual forces of darkness may be working under Satan's direct authority in accordance with the hierarchy.

All the preceding assertions allude to the fact that Satan probably has a well-organized hierarchy in his kingdom. Since humans normally do not see into the spiritual realm, Satan's kingdom may probably be better organized and more efficient than one can imagine. Since there is a well organized hierarchy in the satanic kingdom, demons will definitely take orders from other demons as laid down in the satanic hierarchy. Based on Ephesians 6:12 and the preceding arguments, I strongly support the assertion that Satan has a kingdom and most probably an efficient command hierarchy.

supports the assertion that Satan has probably organized his forces into an army.[2] I believe that there is a well organized army of demons who operate under the directives of the Devil himself.

The High Command Structure of Satan

Do all the demons belong to the four main groups mentioned in Ephesians 6:12? If Satan has probably organized his fighting forces similar to what exists in the army in the physical realm, then the levels in the hierarchy may be more than the four mentioned in Ephesians 6:12. If this assumption is true, then the four levels mentioned, may refer to only the "top command level structure." I believe there may be several levels below the top command level to control the thousands of thousands or millions of demons involved. All the spiritual forces of darkness may be working under Satan's direct authority in accordance with the hierarchy.

All the preceding assertions allude to the fact that Satan probably has a well-organized hierarchy in his kingdom. Since humans normally do not see into the spiritual realm, Satan's kingdom may probably be better organized and more efficient than one can imagine. Since there is a well organized hierarchy in the satanic kingdom, demons will definitely take orders from other demons as laid down in the satanic hierarchy. Based on Ephesians 6:12 and the preceding arguments, I strongly support the assertion that Satan has a kingdom and most probably an efficient command hierarchy.

CHAPTER FIVE

The Nature of Demons

Demons or evil spirits are always evil, wicked, and may dwell in human bodies if permitted. The Scriptures state: "Then he goes and takes with him seven other spirits more wicked than himself, and they enter and dwell there; and the last state of that man is worse than the first…" (Matthew 12:45). Some of these demons may be extremely wicked than others, but all demons are unclean spirits. "And when He had called His disciples to Him, He gave them power over unclean spirits…" (Matthew 10:1).

Demons and Physical Bodies

Demon spirits have no physical bodies of flesh and bones. Jesus said in Luke 24:39 "Behold my hands and my feet, that it is I myself. Handle me and see, for a spirit does not have flesh and bones as you see I have." Jesus was comparing his resurrected body to that of spirits to prove to his disciples that indeed he was resurrected. He had flesh and bones therefore he was not a spirit as the disciples thought. Jesus' explanation may be an indication that it was common knowledge at that time that spirits have no flesh and bones. In the light of Jesus' explanation and Scripture, I support the view that demons do not have physical bodies.

Demons do not possess physical bodies and consequently, they seek to inhabit the bodies of humans or animals. Demons strive to dwell in human bodies in order to manifest or have expression in the physical realm. Luke 8:32-33 says: "Now a herd of many swine was feeding there on the mountain. And they begged him that He would permit them to enter them. And He permitted them. Then the demons went out of the man and entered the swine, and the herd ran violently down the steep place into the lake and drowned." It may be inferred here that the demons were dwelling in the insane man. It is also an indication that the first choice of demons is to inhabit human bodies; but rather than remain without bodies, they may prefer to enter the bodies of animals. This Scripture is also an indication that demons can control the movement and direction of the bodies they inhabit.

From the preceding paragraphs, it is generally accepted that demons do not have physical bodies. However, angels sometimes appear with physical bodies (Genesis 19:1). If indeed demons are fallen angels, why can't they also appear with physical bodies? Has God deprived the fallen angels of the capability to appear with physical bodies? My view is that since demons are fallen angels but do not appear with physical bodies, God has probably deprived them of the capability to appear in the physical realm. This action of God is a great display of his wisdom because if demons are allowed to appear with physical bodies, one can imagine the fear and confusion that they will create among humans in our world.

Marks of Personality of Demons

Despite the fact that demons have no physical bodies, they have all the normally accepted marks of personality such as will, emotion, intellect, self-awareness, and the ability to speak. Mark 5:6-12 states:

> But when he saw Jesus from afar, he ran and worshiped Him. And he cried out with a loud voice

and said, 'What have I to do with You, Jesus, Son of the Most High God? I implore You by God that You do not torment me.' For He said to him, 'Come out of the man, unclean spirit.' Then He asked him 'What is your name?' And he answered saying, 'My name is Legion; for we are many.' And he begged Him earnestly that He would not send them out of the country. Now a large herd of swine was feeding there near the mountains. And all the demons begged Him, saying 'Send us to the swine, that we may enter them.'

In this unique encounter of Jesus with the demonized person, we can deduce the following: (1) the demon used the vocal organs of the victim to express his *will* (I implore you by God that you do not torment me); (2) the demon expressed his *emotion* (And he cried out with a loud voice); (3) the demon expressed his *intellectual* knowledge (What have I to do with you, Jesus, Son of the Most High God?) an indication that the demon knew who Jesus was; (4) the demon had *self-awareness* (My name is Legion; for we are many)—the demons knew who they were, and they had the ability to *speak* using the vocal organs of the victim.

Character Traits of Demons

Demons are supernaturally strong. During my healing and deliverance prayer sessions, I have observed demons manifest a wide range of character traits. Some demons are rather quiet while others may be violent and supernaturally strong. These demonic character traits were displayed by the Gadarene demoniac (Mark 5:3-5, "...no one could bind him, not even with chains...and the chains had been pulled apart by him, and the shackles broken in pieces...crying out and cutting himself with stones"). It may be worth saying here that similar supernatural strength is sometimes displayed by people using certain types of drugs. Someone may probably ask whether there are any demons behind the behavior of those who use hard drugs like cocaine. Probably yes, but this question is outside the scope of this book.

Demons are destructive. Mark 9:21-22 states, "So he asked his father, 'How long has this been happening to him?' And he said from childhood. 'And often he has thrown him both into the fire and into the water to destroy him.'...." Apparently, the demon in this Scripture sought to destroy the life of the boy. Most people refer to this kind of demonic attack as epilepsy. When this demon of epilepsy attacks babies or little children, we refer to it as "convulsion."

Demons are communal *beings*. As communal *beings* they often live and work together. In Matthew 12:43-45, Jesus explains that when a demon is cast out, he goes walking in dry places seeking rest. If he cannot find rest, he comes back to see if the previous habitation is empty. If it is empty, the demon goes to bring seven spirits, extremely more wicked than him to reoccupy the person. Other examples of communal demons are found in Mark 16:9 (Mary's seven demons) and Mark 5:9 (man with a legion of demons).

Capabilities of Demons

Demons can move and travel. What are demons capable of doing? Satan is not omnipresent and therefore he can be present at only one location at a point in time. Consequently, the Devil uses a host of demons, spread out everywhere in the world to do his bidding. Demons have the capability to move about or travel from one point to another very fast. In Matthew 12:43-45: "When an unclean spirit goes out of a man, he goes through dry places...then he goes and takes with him seven other spirits...." It may be inferred here that demons can move about and therefore have the capability to travel. Demons are very busy spirits who virtually never take any rest. It is like they are under intense pressure to accomplish their various assignments right now.

Demons can fight. Demons are capable of fighting with God's angels. Daniel 10:13, 20 states: "But the prince of the kingdom of Persia withstood me twenty-one days; and behold, Michael, one of the chief princes, came to help me....Then he said, do you know why I have come to you? And now I must return to fight with the prince of Persia...." Revelation 12:7 "And war broke out in heaven: Michael and his angels fought against the dragon; and the dragon and his angels fought." These Scripture passages support the assertion that demons have the capability to fight.

Demons Speak in the First Person Singular. Demons are capable of speaking through a person's voice and also see through his eyes. Acts 19:15 states: "And the evil spirit answered and said, 'Jesus I know, and Paul I know, but who are you?'" How do demons speak? Most probably, the demons use the vocal organs of their victims. This may be another indication that demons, most probably, may sometimes enter the human body in order to speak through them. In my own experience in the healing and deliverance ministry, I have heard demons spoke on many occasions using the vocal organs of their victims. These demons, most of the time, speak in the first person singular which makes most people think it is the victim who may be speaking. The Holy Spirit always prompts me to know when it is a demon that is speaking through the human victim.

Demons can invigorate people with extraordinary strength. Acts 19:16 states: "Then the man in whom the evil spirit was leaped on them; overpowering them, and prevailed against them, so that they fled out of that house naked and wounded." Demons, being spirits, can sometimes display extraordinary strength as seen in this Scripture. On a number of occasions, I have witnessed demons manifest violently and resisting their expulsion from a human victim. At one of my prayer meetings in church, a woman manifested so violently that it took four strong men to hold and restrain her. While restraining her, her eye balls changed color to brownish red. I knew it was the demon manifesting, so I commanded that demon to come out in the name of Jesus Christ. The demon screamed and came out and the woman slumped to the floor like a vegetable. The lady was free thereafter. Praise God!

Demons can deceive people. Demons can deceive people and draw them away from the truth of the gospel, enticing them by their own desires. 2 Chronicles 18:20-22 states: "Then a spirit came forward and stood before the Lord, and said, 'I will persuade him?' The Lord said to him, 'In what way?' So he said, 'I will go out and be a lying spirit in the mouth of all his prophets.'...."Acts 5:3 supports the assertion that demons can deceive people to lie: "But Peter said 'Ananias, why has Satan filled your heart to lie to the Holy Spirit and keep back part of the price of the land for yourself?" It may be inferred from Peter's question that the Devil is capable of deceiving people to lie. No wonder Satan is described as the father of lies (John 8:44 states: "..., for he is a liar and the father of it.")

Demons can return to occupy their former victims. In Matthew 12:43-45, we have a classic description of a demon that was expelled but returned later with seven other demons to reoccupy the victim. So what must we do to prevent demons from returning to inhabit our bodies or oppressing us immediately we are delivered? As soon as you are liberated from demons, you must stay close to Jesus, attend Church services regularly, read the Bible and pray daily, and above all, always confess that you have been liberated in the name of Jesus Christ. You must also confess all the time that Jesus Christ is your Lord and Savior and that you have nothing to do with Satan. Remember there is power in this type of confession to keep Satan and his cohorts away from you.

CHAPTER SIX

Demons in the Old and New Testaments

The Old Testament is virtually silent on activities of demons when compared with the New Testament. What could be the reason for this unusual silence of demonic activity in the Old Testament? Is it because demons were not active, or they were active but no one could recognize their activities? One major difference between the Old and New Testaments is that, while there is no record of deliverances from evil spirits in the Old Testament, right from the time that Jesus proclaimed the kingdom of God, many evil spirits were cast out of many people.

Satan appeared in the Garden of Eden to tempt Adam and Eve (Genesis 3), and thereafter appeared again before God and asked for permission to tempt Job (Job 1-2). There were few instances of demonic activities mentioned in the Old Testament, for example, when Saul was tormented by an evil spirit; and David was enlisted in Saul's court to play the harp (1 Samuel 16:14-16). Satan accused Job and also accused God (Job 1-2).

Demons were indeed virtually inactive in the Old Testament when compared to the New Testament. Could it also be that the Devil had the majority of people under his influence, so demons were not harassing them? Could it also be that the main aim of Satan and his cohorts is to prevent human beings from receiving salvation through Christ? If the latter was true, then it explains why demonic activities erupted among humans just when Jesus Christ proclaimed the kingdom of God and preached the salvation message.

We have a record of numerous references to evil spirits in the New Testament. It appears that the people knew about the existence of demons, as there were several reports about how they oppressed people and sought to destroy others. It may also be inferred that when the Devil appeared openly to tempt Jesus in the desert (Matthew 4:1-11), the former, thereafter, launched a full scale attack on humanity. This became evident as Jesus cast out many demons to set many people free.

The existence of Satan was established right from the beginning of the Old Testament (Genesis 3:1). It is also clear that a spirit *being* spoke through a serpent to Eve in Genesis 3 and caused the Fall of humanity into sin. Lucifer was an angel in heaven when man was created. From the day Lucifer was expelled from heaven to become the Devil on this Earth, he had since sought to destroy humanity. My view is that, although there were fewer demonic activities in the Old Testament, the main difference is that there was no record of deliverances of people from demons in the Old Testament. However, in the New Testament, we see a lot of people being set free from demons. This indeed is the beginning of a new dispensation and an indication that Jesus Christ has truly delegated His authority to believers in these latter days to destroy the work of the Devil.

We have a lot of evidence to the reality of demons in the New Testament. The New Testament (especially the Gospels and the Acts of the Apostles) records a significant number of instances of demonic activities. Wherever the gospel was preached, demons were cast out and many people were healed (Mark 1:32-34, 5:1-18, 9:14-29). With the appearance of Jesus Christ on the world scene, activities of demons suddenly came to the forefront. Thanks to God for the light that Jesus brought into the world to expose the activities of Satan and his cohorts.

CHAPTER SEVEN

The Origin of Human Illness

Where did human illness originate? The general cause of human illness is the sin of Adam and Eve which resulted in the Fall that has affected all creation. Consequently, human illness originated from the original sin of Adam and Eve when they disobeyed God's commandment (Genesis 3:6-7). This original sin of Adam and Eve caused humanity to experience spiritual death, brought disease and sickness, and eventual physical death. Therefore sin, disease and death became part of the consequences of man's disobedience of God's commandment.

It may be assumed that Adam and Eve lived in the Garden of Eden for a number of years before they disobeyed God and sinned. This assumption also presupposes that Satan had the capability to inflict disease and sickness on man prior to the Fall but could not do it because the perfect sinless bodies of Adam and Eve were probably resistant to diseases. Psalm 139:14a states: "I will praise You, for I am fearfully and wonderfully made." In this case, it may also be assumed that it was sin that destroyed any natural immunity against diseases that might have been in the body of man prior to the Fall. Consequently, it may be inferred that it was sin that opened the way for Satan to attack humans with sickness and disease.

The Devil certainly has a lot to do with human sicknesses. The Scriptures declare that Satan went out from the presence of the Lord to strike Job with painful boils (Job 2:7). This Scripture probably substantiates the assertion that Satan may be the author of all sickness because there is no record of sickness in heaven. It may also be concluded that every misfortune that causes pain must be from the Devil.

Other Causes of Human Illness

What are the other causes of diseases? As mentioned in the preceding paragraphs, sin resulting in the Fall of man is the main cause of disease. That notwithstanding, there are a number of other possible causes of human illness:

1. **Physical causes.** Medical science has taught us that micro-organisms such as viruses and bacteria or improper diet may cause an illness.
2. **Harmful personal habits.** When someone takes in certain harmful drugs like cocaine, it may have direct physical consequences resulting in sickness.
3. **Demons.** Demons may be responsible for certain illnesses. I believe that demons may inhabit and control a person's will for their selfish purpose of doing their will in the physical realm, and to destroy and torment their victims physically, spiritually, and mentally.
4. **God.** Once a while, an illness may also have its primary source in God to fulfill a purpose of God. Some people may have a lot of questions why an illness may be allowed by God. But the Scriptures have references in support of these assertions. John 9:1-3 states: "Now as Jesus passed by, He saw a man who was blind from birth. And His disciples asked Him, saying 'Rabbi, who sinned, this man or his parents that he was born blind?'" Jesus answered "Neither this man nor his parents sinned, but that the works of God should be revealed in him."

The disciples thought that the man's blindness was due to sin, but Jesus explained that the blindness was not due to sin but it was allowed to bring glory to God's name. This may also be an indication that it was common knowledge that sin could be the cause of sickness at the time of Jesus. In the Old Testament, the Lord smote the king, so that he became a leper to the day of his death (2 Kings 15:5). So also in Daniel 4:28-37, the Lord struck King Nebuchadnezzar with insanity to discipline him.

5. **Violation of health regulations.** Other causes of diseases may be due to violation of health regulations, as when people live in unhygienic environment.

According to John M. Last:

There is a direct relationship between filth and diseases. The phrase "filth diseases" was coined in 1858 by a British physician, Charles Murchison, to describe a class of conditions, mostly caused by infectious pathogens, that were associated with squalid living conditions—the overcrowded, unsanitary, and vermin-infested dwellings that were all too numerous in urban areas in the nineteenth century.[1]

Medical science has taught us that sickness may be caused by germs. In everyday life, humans may be sick from bacteria and viruses and not because the Devil or demons have attacked them.

CHAPTER EIGHT

Are Demons the Cause of Every Sickness?

The Scriptures clearly recognize that some illnesses are not attributable to demons. Jesus healed all diseases and delivered those who were demonized. Mark 1:32- 34 states: "Now at evening when the sun had set, they brought to Him all who were sick and those who were demon-possessed....Then He healed many who were sick with various diseases, and cast out many demons;...." In this Scripture, it is clear that Jesus *healed many who had various diseases,* and He also *cast out many demons.*

There is a Difference between Healing and Deliverance

Luke 9:1 states: "Then He called His twelve disciples together and gave them power and authority over all demons, and to cure diseases." In Luke 9:1, Jesus gave authority to his twelve disciples in two dimensions: (1) to cast out demons and (2) to heal diseases. Demons are cast out from humans in the name of Jesus Christ while diseases are healed in the name of Jesus Christ. The Scriptures clearly indicate here that certain diseases may be caused by demons while others may not have any demonic cause. Therefore, the Scriptures are abundantly clear that there is a difference between *healing* and *deliverance* from evil spirits.

The Scriptures make it clear that some illnesses are not attributable to demons because Jesus sent this message to Herod: "...I cast out demons and perform cures..." (Luke 13:32). Based on this Scripture and in my own personal experience in the healing and deliverance ministry, I support the view that demons are not the cause of every illness. I have laid my hands on sick people, prayed for them and they were healed. In other instances, I had to cast out a demon for healing to occur.

When are Demons the Cause of a Sickness?

If demons are not the cause of every sickness, then how do we determine when a demon is the cause of a particular sickness? It is evident from the Scriptures that demons may cause a variety of symptoms (physical, mental and spiritual). It is also abundantly clear that these same symptoms may be the result of other causes other than demons. Most of the time, it may be a combination of causes, most probably natural and supernatural. I strongly support the assertion that Scripture makes a distinction between natural and demonic causes of physical and mental illnesses.

So what symptoms do we look for in order to determine whether a demon is the cause of a particular illness? In my own ministry, when someone comes in sick and says that the doctors have no clue and the specialists have given up, my first reaction is to attack demons and cast them out. All that notwithstanding, I have found out in my ministry that the surest way to know whether there is a demon behind a sickness is by the Holy Spirit gift of discerning of spirits. However, when the sickness or the pain persists, and even when I am not sure that it is being caused by a demon, I just go ahead to attack demons and cast them out in the name of Jesus Christ. On many occasions this method has proved successful as the victims were healed.

A Strange Behavior May be a Sign of Demonization

I always suspect demonic influence of an illness when there is strange behavior or when there is a change of voice in speech or laughter of the victim, especially during deliverance prayer sessions. When demons are involved in the sickness, especially in cases of demonization, there is something strange about the eyes when the victim manifests. The eyes of the demonized are most of the time brownish red or exceptionally bright and bulging out of the sockets. This is normally the situation when the demon is manifesting through the victim. Any violent struggle with extraordinary strength is also an indication of a demonic manifestation.

The above-mentioned behaviors or characteristics may be observed in severely demonized people. Some of these behaviors may also be found in common with mental sickness. However, it must be cautioned that the observation of only one of the foregoing behaviors may not be a conclusive indication of demon presence or activity. Some of these symptoms may not even be clearly defined, which makes it difficult to determine whether the sickness is demonic or not. However, these behaviors are acceptable guidelines in determining whether an illness is demonic or not. Pastors involved in the healing and deliverance ministry see these manifestations so often and are therefore able to identify them quickly.

CHAPTER NINE

Strange Causes of Illnesses

It is an open secret that with the advancement in medical science, humanity knows a lot more today about the natural causes of human illnesses; and pharmacology has contributed a lot to their cure. However, there are still many sicknesses and diseases currently attacking humanity for several decades now for which no explanations or complete cures have really been found. For example, cancer and AIDS (Acquired Immune Deficiency Syndrome). One may also see certain abnormal behaviors in humans which medical science does not seem to have explanations or cures. Could there be some supernatural causes to such sicknesses?

Many people may not believe there are supernatural or demonic causes to certain illnesses but from my experience in ministry, I know for sure that there are such causes although not easy to explain. In this modern scientific era, the diagnosis of a disease is done on the natural level without recourse to the supernatural realm. This has been the trend because Medical doctors are trained to diagnose sickness in the physical realm only, and therefore they do not delve into any supernatural causes.

What are the causes of these strange illnesses? The Scriptures may be the best source for these causes:

1. In Matthew 9:32-33, they brought to Jesus, a man who was demonized and mute; and when the demon was cast out, the mute spoke. What has the demon got to do with the man's inability to speak? Since this man has not been speaking for quite some time, may be a couple of days, a couple of weeks or months or even years, it is reasonable to infer that the demon may be the cause. Someone may argue that it was probably a coincidence. That may be true, but when coincidences become a regular pattern, then a reasonable mind is compelled to conclude otherwise.
2. In Luke 13:11-13, a woman who had a spirit of infirmity eighteen years, and was bent over came to Jesus. Jesus said to her: "Woman, you are loosed from

your infirmity." The woman was made straight when Jesus laid his hands upon her. When the woman was set free from the spirit of infirmity, she was made straight. In these instances when the demons were cast out, the victims were healed. Therefore, it may be reasonable to infer that the demons were the causes of their problems.

3. Mark 5:3-4 states: "who had his dwelling among the tombs; and no one could bind him, not even with chains, because he had often been bound with shackles and chains. And the chains had been pulled apart by him, and the shackles broken in pieces...." This man displayed extraordinary strength to break shackles. There must be a source for this extraordinary strength which may be attributed to the demons controlling him (v. 8-9).

4. **Strange Antisocial behaviors**. The man in Mark 5: 1-15 displayed strange antisocial behaviors such as self-inflicted wounds, nakedness, and screaming. The man's condition was such that he could no longer live among the people in the community. It is highly probable that he was under the influence of demons because when the demons left, he

became sober and normal (v.15). It is also probable that it was the demons that caused him to move out of the community.

5. **Mental and emotional problems.** There are various degrees of mental illness. Depression is one level of a mental or emotional problem. In Mark 9: 14-27, the epileptic boy was demonized. When Jesus commanded the demon to leave, the boy was thrown down in violent convulsions, apparently caused by the demon. When the demon left, the boy was healed and behaved normally.

All the sicknesses described above appear out of the ordinary, and certainly may have causes which may be deeper than meets the eye. Are demons responsible for such illnesses? I know there are psychological or physical explanations for illness. However, I wish to emphasize the fact that more frequently than many believers realize, the cause may be demonic.

CHAPTER TEN

Role of Demons in Illness

If demons are behind certain illnesses, what role do they play? Looking at all things from the view in the physical realm, it may be difficult for many people to imagine how a demon can inflict human bodies with sicknesses. However, most people in my town and villages in my tribal areas in Africa know that demons are the cause of human mental problems and strange illnesses. Interestingly, I have come to know that most Europeans and Americans find it hard to believe that demons can affect human bodies, causing physical disability and sickness. May God help all of us to grasp this truth that demons are real spirit *beings* who interfere in the lives of humans in one way or the other. Every activity of demons is directed towards humans to damage or destroy the latter (John 10:10).

Activities in the Spiritual Realm Control Activities in the Physical Realm

Satan and demons have the capability to attack humans from the spiritual realm to inflict the latter with all kinds of diseases. It is amazing to know that an activity in the spiritual realm controls occurrences in the physical realm. Whatever we see happen in the physical realm has already been concluded in the spiritual realm. In this sense it seems the spiritual realm controls the physical realm. Job 2:7 states: "Then Satan went out from the presence of the Lord, and struck Job with painful boils from the sole of his foot to the crown of his head." Satan virtually carried the sickness in the spiritual realm and placed them on Job, and it manifested in the physical realm on the latter's body. I wish to emphasize the fact that the real powers behind our physical world are spiritual in nature.

Demons may influence and afflict human bodies from within when they enter any part of the human body. These demons may cause poor heart or blood pressure problems. I also believe that demons are the cause of all forms of cancer and that is why for all these decades, no cure has been found yet. Demons are known to cause many physical ailments such as muteness (Matthew 9:32-33), blindness (Matthew 12:22); and many other defects and painful deformities (Luke 13:11-17).

Duties of Individual Demons

What are the duties of individual demons in the satanic kingdom? From our earlier discussion of the satanic kingdom, it was established that there is a hierarchy. Every demon operates at its own level under a superior demon, and each demon is assigned a specific duty or task. Demons subsequently adopt the name of the duty they perform as their name. There are demons of adultery, fornication, filthy works, depression, quarrelsome, anger, laziness, gossip, etc. Every negative behavior of human beings which are the works of the flesh (Galatians 5:19-21) is influenced by demons while every positive behavior is influenced by the Holy Spirit as the fruit of the Holy Spirit (Galatians 5:22-23).

Every Individual Demon can perform only one job— therefore they are specialists on their jobs

Adultery is a spirit, meaning there may be a demon behind an adulterous behavior of any human being. Whenever such a spirit enters a human body or life, it may cause the person to want to commit adultery and it will be in the form of a strong temptation. Each spirit has his area of specialization and that a spirit of adultery may not cause deafness. The following are some duties which demons may perform and therefore adopt these duties as their names:

1. Spirit of infirmity (Luke 13:11)
2. Dumb spirit (Mark 9:25)
3. Deaf spirit (Mark 9:25)
4. Distressing spirit (1 Samuel 16:14)
5. Unclean spirit (Matthew 10:1)
6. Spirit of divination (Acts 16:16)
7. Spirit of bondage (Romans 8:15)
8. Deceiving spirits (1Timothy 4:1)
9. Spirit of jealousy (Numbers 5:14)
10. Spirit of fear (2 Timothy 1:7)
11. Sorrowful spirit (1 Samuel 1:15)
12. Spirit of harlotry (Hosea 4:12)

Spirit of Fear

An example from my own ministry is on the spirit of fear. A couple of years ago a lady was brought to church on a Sunday morning. Her story was that she could no longer drive her car because each time she sat behind her steering wheel in the car there was a strange fear that came upon her. On two occasions, she was so scared that she was involved in accidents. On hearing her story, I knew she was being tormented by a spirit of fear. I said "God has not given us a spirit of fear, but of power and of love and of a sound mind" (2 Timothy 1:7). As I prayed for her, I commanded the spirit of fear to leave. She slumped to the floor and remained there a couple of minutes. The deliverance was instant as she gave testimony to her freedom. We give the glory to Jesus.

Many years ago in Ghana, a little baby about ten months old was brought to Church during our evening service. The baby was crying at the top of her voice. According to the mother the baby has been crying continuously night and day for almost two days. When they took her to the hospital the doctors could not find anything wrong and yet the baby kept crying. When I saw the child the Holy Spirit revealed to me that the baby was being tormented by a spirit of fear in a very strange manner. I prayed and commanded that spirit to come out and to stop interfering in the life of the child. Instantly and I mean instantly, the child stopped crying and I gave her back to the mother. I still remember that evening like it was yesterday. We thank God for everything and the authority that Jesus has delegated to believers to destroy the work of the devil.

Demons that cause severe pain in the human body

There are demons that cause severe pain in the human body. Medical science is unable to diagnose the cause of such pain. About five years ago, this young man in his early forties was introduced to me. He was suffering from a very severe pain in both legs. He was not working because of the pain. He said he had seen all the specialists and all the medications proved futile during the previous six weeks. I told him that the pain was probably being caused by a demon. I started praying with him daily because his home was just about ten minutes drive from my home. By the seventh day all the demons causing the pain left and he jumped up strong and healthy. Nobody could believe that what medications could not accomplish, in the name of Jesus it was done. Praise God!

Recently, the spouse of one of my female members also suffered from severe waist pains. He felt the pain severely at night although he felt it during the day also. He was never able to sleep at night. They tried all kinds of medications to no avail. The woman informed me that the husband's condition was getting worse so I declared three days of fasting and prayer. On the first day, we went to pray and commanded the demon causing the pain to leave. To our pleasant surprise the gentleman was able to sleep soundly for the first time in several weeks. That was his deliverance and healing. We give all the glory to Jesus in whose name we exercise authority over demons and destroy their work. If you have a chronic pain in your body and all the known medications for pain fail to bring relief, the cause may be demonic. Seek the help of a pastor in the healing and deliverance ministry.

CHAPTER ELEVEN

Mental Illness

What is mental illness? "Mental illness (or emotional disability, cognitive dysfunction) is a broad generic label for a category of illnesses that may include affective or emotional instability, behavioral deregulation, and/or cognitive dysfunction or impairment."[1] "Specific illnesses known as mental illnesses include major depression, generalized anxiety disorder, schizophrenia, and attention deficit hyperactivity disorder."[2]

Although medical science has taught us that some "mental illness" may be caused by physical deficiencies such as a chemical imbalance in the brain that can be treated by medication, there is a "mental illness" that is caused by demons. Diane Dew supports this view as follows: "Other 'mental illnesses' are caused by demons, and no amount of medication or psychological therapy or psychiatric treatment can help—only spiritual deliverance can set the person free."[3] How can someone identify mental illness caused by physical deficiencies and mental illness caused by demons? The symptoms and behavior of the victims may be similar.

Throughout the gospels, Jesus Christ healed many illnesses, especially mental illness caused by demonization. Jesus healed these mental illnesses by casting out demons from their victims. The import of this observation is that certain mental illnesses may be caused by demons which cannot be treated by medication except by exorcism in the name of Jesus Christ. However, other mental illnesses caused by physical deficiencies may be treatable by medication and/or psychological therapy. In the case of the Gadarene demoniac when demons were involved, the victim may resort to violence and may at times display extraordinary strength. Such a victim could only be healed by spiritual deliverance in the name of Jesus Christ.

What are the symptoms of a mental illness? We may say that the Gadarene demoniac was suffering from a mental illness. In that sense let us examine his condition in Mark 5:1-9:

1. He had his dwelling among the tombs (v.3a). This may be an indication that he was antisocial. The demon was probably in control of his life and drove him out of the city.
2. No one could bind him, not even with chains (v.3b), and he could break shackles and pull chains apart easily (v.4). This is an indication that he possessed a supernatural strength which most probably came from the demons.
3. He lived in the mountains, crying out and cutting himself with stones (v.5). This may be an indication that he had the tendency to harm himself and it is not likely that someone in his right mind could do that to himself.

The assertion that demons may be the cause of certain mental illnesses, including schizophrenia, is supported by Dr. Terry Vanover, MD.[4]

From the preceding paragraphs, it may be concluded that demons may be the cause of certain mental illnesses. This is also substantiated by the story of the Gadarene demoniac (Mark 5:1-18).

Schizophrenia is definitely demonic

One day a lady came to talk to me about her daughter who appeared to be suffering from some type of depression. She intimated that her daughter's depression probably started about two years earlier but they did not recognize it. I asked the lady to describe the daughter's behavior. She said to me: "Pastor, for several months now, my daughter who lives alone in another part of the city, behaves queerly." I asked her what she meant by queerly. The lady continued: "My daughter isolates herself from everybody. She does not call again like she used to do and even when we call her she does not answer her cell phone."

As I listened attentively, the lady continued: "We were very concerned about her rather abnormal behavior. When we finally made personal contact with her, we were shocked by her complaints. My daughter said some people like the FBI personnel have been shadowing her and wherever she goes these secret agents took pictures of her." The lady said at that juncture she concluded that something was seriously wrong with her daughter who was in her middle thirties. The lady said her daughter also intimated that her cell phone calls were being tapped so she changed her phone numbers every three or four days.

The lady started sobbing when I interrupted her. I told her that her daughter was suffering from schizophrenia, a higher form of depression caused by demons. I also told her that medical science has no cure for it and that the only sure cure is by a prayer of deliverance in the name of Jesus Christ. I explained to her that her daughter's strange behavior was being caused by demons and all we needed to do was to cast these demons out in the name of Jesus Christ. I scheduled with this lady to pay an unannounced visit to her daughter the following Saturday in the morning.

By the grace of God we met her in the house. After a short exchange of greetings, I began to pray for her deliverance. I commanded the demons involved to leave in the name of Jesus. Within fifteen minutes from the time we stepped into the house, this woman, suffering from schizophrenia was free. The demons did not manifest, they just ceased interfering in the young woman's life and left. She came to church the following day, Sunday, to worship with us. It is my pleasure to say to the glory of the Lord Jesus that the young woman is still worshipping with us and leading a normal life. Thank you Jesus, for great things you have done! I fully support the conclusion of Dr. Terry Vanover that schizophrenia is definitely demonic.

CHAPTER TWELVE

Why do Demons Love to Inhabit Humans?

We established in an earlier chapter that demons are disembodied fallen spirits that crave to inhabit humans. Why do these spirits love to inhabit humans? One obvious reason why demons seek habitation in human bodies is to enable them manifest themselves in the physical realm. It is easier for demons to accomplish their purposes when they dwell in a human body. The purposes of demons are always damaging and destructive to humans. John 10:10 states "The thief does not come except to steal, and to kill, and to destroy...."

Demons use every means to cause man to sin and turn him away from God. I am fully convinced that as fallen spirits, demons desire to dwell in human bodies in order to manifest themselves. For example, the man in the synagogue tormented by an unclean spirit (Mark. 1:21-28). When demons inhabit human bodies, it is easier for them to fulfill their master's mission. Satan's mission is to steal, kill and destroy (John 10:10). Likewise, demons will try to steal, kill and destroy whatever they can. Demons will sometimes try to block or thwart the efforts of God's servants to prevent them from fulfilling their destinies. They do this by bringing upon God's servants depression, temptation, doubt, sickness and sometimes accidents, etc.

When demons cannot get habitation in a human body they prefer animals, even swine as opposed to just roaming about (Mark 5:12). We know that human beings are the prime targets of demons, therefore the latter prefer to inhabit the former in order to accomplish Satan's purposes.

How do Demons Inhabit Humans?

Demonic Doorways. What rights have demons to enter humans and how do they do that? Demons gain access to people in a variety of ways also known as demonic *doorways*. According to Dua-Agyeman: "People come under the influence of evil powers through *demonic doorways* that provide demons with the *legal right* to intrude upon one's life and circumstances."[1] What are *demonic doorways?* These are spiritual doorways or gates through which demons gain entrance into human lives.

Sin and Curses open Major Demonic Doorways

Sin and curses open major demonic doorways that give demons the legal right to enter human bodies or lives. Sexual sins such as adultery, fornication and filthy works offer evil spirits strong footholds to oppress those involved. Sin being a major doorway, Jesus told the sick man "go and sin no more, lest a worse thing come upon you" (John 5:5-14). Even sins of omission and commission may open doors for demons to enter a human life. Demons are always craving to enter human beings therefore any act of sin that breaks a man's relationship with the Lord Jesus Christ opens a door for demons to enter. In such cases the demons either enter the human body or oppress him from outside.

Demons in Little Children

Sometimes demons enter little children from the day they were born or very early in their childhood. This happens when the parents approve or open a door for the particular demon to enter. This deal may be accomplished through a to manifest themselves. For example, the man in the synagogue tormented by an unclean spirit (Mark. 1:21-28). When demons inhabit human bodies, it is easier for them to fulfill their master's mission. Satan's mission is to steal, kill and destroy (John 10:10). Likewise, demons will try to steal, kill and destroy whatever they can. Demons will sometimes try to block or thwart the efforts of God's servants to prevent them from fulfilling their destinies. They do this by bringing upon God's servants depression, temptation, doubt, sickness and sometimes accidents, etc.

When demons cannot get habitation in a human body they prefer animals, even swine as opposed to just roaming about (Mark 5:12). We know that human beings are the prime targets of demons, therefore the latter prefer to inhabit the former in order to accomplish Satan's purposes.

How do Demons Inhabit Humans?

Demonic Doorways. What rights have demons to enter humans and how do they do that? Demons gain access to people in a variety of ways also known as demonic *doorways*. According to Dua-Agyeman: "People come under the influence of evil powers through *demonic doorways* that provide demons with the *legal right* to intrude upon one's life and circumstances."[1] What are *demonic doorways?* These are spiritual doorways or gates through which demons gain entrance into human lives.

Sin and Curses open Major Demonic Doorways

Sin and curses open major demonic doorways that give demons the legal right to enter human bodies or lives. Sexual sins such as adultery, fornication and filthy works offer evil spirits strong footholds to oppress those involved. Sin being a major doorway, Jesus told the sick man "go and sin no more, lest a worse thing come upon you" (John 5:5-14). Even sins of omission and commission may open doors for demons to enter a human life. Demons are always craving to enter human beings therefore any act of sin that breaks a man's relationship with the Lord Jesus Christ opens a door for demons to enter. In such cases the demons either enter the human body or oppress him from outside.

Demons in Little Children

Sometimes demons enter little children from the day they were born or very early in their childhood. This happens when the parents approve or open a door for the particular demon to enter. This deal may be accomplished through a covenant or some kind of agreement with the Devil. The most common demon is the spirit of witchcraft. Normally by the time these children are about four or five years old, they are taught to 'fly' and begin to go on errands with older witches. Such children are jittery and scared in the presence of the Holy Spirit anointing.

One Sunday afternoon, during my healing and deliverance service, I observed something strange that I have never observed before. Towards the end of the service and led by the Holy Spirit, I started walking among the congregation when my eyes fell on a little child sitting on the laps of a woman. This little boy was about two years old. Immediately my eyes made contact with his eyes, the boy started screaming at the top of his voice. As I moved closer to him, he screamed even louder and covered his face with his two palms and shouting "no, no, no." The creaming was so loud that it drew the attention of virtually everyone in the Sanctuary.

Later on, the lady who brought the little boy to church told me that throughout the two-hour service, the little boy never allowed them to stay in the sanctuary. The boy either pretended he wanted to use the bathroom or wanted to eat. It was during the last twenty minutes of the service that the lady said she ignored the excuses of the boy and came into the sanctuary. The lady also said that during their short stay in the sanctuary, each time I passed by their isle, the boy behaved rather queerly but she never understood it until I came close and he started screaming. The boy was screaming because the demon in him had recognized the Holy Spirit in me and could not stand the anointing fire.

Why not cast the Demon out?

Although I knew by the Holy Spirit that the boy was demonized, it might interest you to know that I made no attempt to cast out that spirit. I rather requested that the biological mother should be informed about what happened and if she was interested, she should bring the boy for deliverance. You may be wondering why I wanted the mother herself to bring the boy to the deliverance prayer meeting. Since the mother knew how the spirit entered the boy, she must be present to confess that they do not want that spirit in the boy again. Demons are very legalistic and may at times refer you to a covenant or an agreement that they have entered into with the victim or family. Surprisingly, the mother never showed up till today which was an indication that she knew how that spirit entered the boy and she wanted to retain the status quo. It is a pity how some parents enslave their own children before they grow into adults.

CHAPTER THIRTEEN

Is it Demon Possession or Demonization?

For a very long time, there has been so much debate among theologians on the use of the words *demonization* and *demon possession* to describe a particular sick human condition when demons are involved. In order to try to resolve the issue, it is pertinent to look at the etymology of *demonization* and its usage in the New Testament. The Greek verb *daimonizomai* means "to be possessed by a demon."[1] A close analysis of the Greek word *daimonizomenos* leads to the conclusion that the correct word to use is *demonization* and not *demon possession*.

Unfortunately, some Bible versions have translated the Greek word as "demon possessed" which has created the confusion in the usage of the correct word, "demonized."

Demonization is appropriately described as a demon inhabiting a human body.

My opinion on the use of the words *demonization* and *demon possession* is that some theologians probably may be using the two words interchangeably to describe the same human condition. However, we now know that the phrase "demon possession" was not used at all in the original Greek manuscripts of the Bible. In this case someone may ask how and when did the phrase "demon possession" appear in some of the versions of the Holy Bible? For example, Mark 1:23, "Just then a man in their synagogue who was *possessed* by an evil spirit cried out" (NIV). I believe the error was due to inaccurate translation of the Greek manuscripts into the English language. Looking at the meanings of the following Greek words may also help to identify the correct word:

- *Daimonion echon.* One having a demon or bearing a demon within oneself. The use of this word implies physical and mental torture.
- *Daimonizomai.* It means *to be demonized.* It has the idea of control or influence over the victim. A control which the victim cannot resist.

- *Ochloumenous. It means one being tormented by evil (unclean) spirits.* The use of this word implies a torture being wrought by the evil spirit.

In line with the meanings of the three Greek words given above, I support the earlier assertion that *possession* is being used incorrectly instead of *demonization*. Some theologians believe that the word *possessed* does not bring out the exact meaning of the Greek word which would be better translated *demonized* or "had a demon."

I believe that in demonization, the personality of the demon overshadows the personality of the victim. Consequently, the demon manifests his personality through the victim's body and this is the reason why the work the demon performs becomes the behavior of the victim. In my view the correct word to describe a person who "has a demon" is *demonization*. The Greek word *daimonizomenoi* is better translated "demonized" (Matthew 4:24; Mark 1:32; Luke 8:36). Any person who is demonized is also being influenced, afflicted, or tormented in some way by that demonic spirit.

CHAPTER FOURTEEN

Physical Manifestations of Demons

How do demons manifest themselves in the physical realm when in reality they are disembodied spirits? As discussed earlier, demons crave to enter human bodies in order to manifest themselves in the physical realm. Without human bodies, demons may find it virtually impossible to manifest themselves physically. During my healing and deliverance prayer meetings, I have observed all kinds of demonic manifestations. The most common is a twitching or contortion on the face of the victim. Sometimes the eye balls may roll upwards showing only the white portion and at times the victim may spin around.

Demonic Manifestations may be seen in Bodily Movements and Facial Contortions

The most identifiable manifestation of demons may be observed in a severely demonized person. An example of this manifestation is seen in the Gadarene demoniac (Mark 5:1-20). Most other manifestations are observed in demonized people when the power of the Holy Spirit is present through his anointing. The majority of these manifestations are observed in bodily movements and facial contortions.

On a number of occasions at my prayer meetings, I have heard demons screamed and came out of their victims. "And when the unclean spirit had convulsed him and cried out with a loud voice, he came out of him" (Mark 1:26); "and always, night and day, he was in the mountains and in the tombs, crying out and cutting himself with stones" (Mark 5:5). I have observed at one of my meetings a woman who slumped to the floor and began slithering like a snake.

It is interesting to note that these manifestations are the same, no matter where and when. A snake spirit manifests in the same manner everywhere through the victim. This goes to prove that it is a particular spirit that manifests. Some of these manifestations are frightening at times. I remember a lady who manifested once in church during a prayer meeting. Her face suddenly and briefly changed to something more like an animal's face which initially scared me. Sometimes, severe demonization manifests in the form of insanity like the Gadarene demoniac. These manifestations are caused by the movements of the demon spirits inside the bodies of the victims or from outside in the form of oppression.

Demons are identified with serpents, "and the great dragon was cast out, that old serpent, called the Devil, and Satan, which deceives the whole world" (Revelation 12:9). In line with this Scripture, it is not surprising that sometimes, serpentine manifestations are witnessed at deliverance sessions. These manifestations may be in the tongue which may cause the tongue of the victim to go in and out very rapidly and exactly like a snake's tongue.

At one of my meetings recently, a woman manifested a serpent in a different manner. How do I know it was a serpent? Although, the woman was standing upright and her head was slightly bent forward, the eyes were protruding with a strange reddish brown color. The tongue was longer than I thought normal and she was projecting it, in and out of the mouth at a very rapid rate, something the woman could not have done on her own. My assistants helping me with the deliverance who saw it knew the woman was behaving like a snake. Finally, as I commanded that spirit to come out, the woman screamed and fell to the floor. She was down on the floor quietly as opposed to the way she was struggling at the beginning. When she got up, she was delivered. We give all the glory to God.

Sometimes, demon manifestations may produce a change in the tone of the human voice. It appears most of these physical manifestations may only be observed when the people are demonized; or when they are severely oppressed and the anointing power of the Holy Spirit is present during a prayer session.

Do all Demons Manifest?

I have observed in my ministry that all demons do not manifest physically before they come out of their victims. An example is a demon of alcoholism. Several years ago I prayed for a young man who was in his thirties and has been an alcoholic for a couple of years in the African nation of Ghana. When he was brought to me, he looked more like an insane man. He was very dirty with an offensive stench emanating from his body because he had not had a shower prayer meeting. Her face suddenly and briefly changed to something more like an animal's face which initially scared me. Sometimes, severe demonization manifests in the form of insanity like the Gadarene demoniac. These manifestations are caused by the movements of the demon spirits inside the bodies of the victims or from outside in the form of oppression.

Demons are identified with serpents, "and the great dragon was cast out, that old serpent, called the Devil, and Satan, which deceives the whole world" (Revelation 12:9). In line with this Scripture, it is not surprising that sometimes, serpentine manifestations are witnessed at deliverance sessions. These manifestations may be in the tongue which may cause the tongue of the victim to go in and out very rapidly and exactly like a snake's tongue.

At one of my meetings recently, a woman manifested a serpent in a different manner. How do I know it was a serpent? Although, the woman was standing upright and her head was slightly bent forward, the eyes were protruding with a strange reddish brown color. The tongue was longer than I thought normal and she was projecting it, in and out of the mouth at a very rapid rate, something the woman could not have done on her own. My assistants helping me with the deliverance who saw it knew the woman was behaving like a snake. Finally, as I commanded that spirit to come out, the woman screamed and fell to the floor. She was down on the floor quietly as opposed to the way she was struggling at the beginning. When she got up, she was delivered. We give all the glory to God.

Sometimes, demon manifestations may produce a change in the tone of the human voice. It appears most of these physical manifestations may only be observed when the people are demonized; or when they are severely oppressed and the anointing power of the Holy Spirit is present during a prayer session.

Do all Demons Manifest?

I have observed in my ministry that all demons do not manifest physically before they come out of their victims. An example is a demon of alcoholism. Several years ago I prayed for a young man who was in his thirties and has been an alcoholic for a couple of years in the African nation of Ghana. When he was brought to me, he looked more like an insane man. He was very dirty with an offensive stench emanating from his body because he had not had a shower for several days. When he sat down, he would neither talk nor lift up his head.

The Holy Spirit prompted me to read aloud the story of the Gadarene Demoniac (Mark 5:1-18). After reading the Scripture, I prayed and commanded the demon of alcoholism to leave in the name of Jesus. Instantly, the young man lifted his head up and I knew that the demon spirit had left. I asked him whether he would like a cup of tea or coffee. To my pleasant surprise, he said he wanted to go home for a shower. I said, "Praise the Lord." I gave him a ride home and asked him to come to my open air crusade that evening. He turned up that evening and all those who knew him were amazed to see him so well dressed. We give the glory to God, for great things he has done.

Demons that use Deception to Evade Expulsion

Some demons sometimes use clever strategies to evade expulsion from their victims. I have observed this class of demons manifest in the same manner on several occasions at my deliverance prayer meetings. However, it took me quite some time to learn from the Holy Spirit what these demons were up to. What these demons do is that before the pastor gets close to their victim, they cause the person to slump to the floor as if the Holy Spirit has knocked them down. Once the person is on the floor, naturally, the pastor's attention is directed away from them, which is what most of us pastors do. When pastors turn away from such a victim, he or she eventually gets up when no one is watching and the demon has thus evaded expulsion. Having known this strategy of some demons, I always follow such victims to the floor and command the demons out in the name of Jesus Christ.

CHAPTER FIFTEEN

Can Demons Indwell Christians?

One of the major questions that has engaged the attention of theologians for several decades is "whether demons can indwell Christians?" This question has generated a lot of debate and has even created a dichotomy among theologians. There are those who assert that demons can indwell the bodies of only unbelievers; and there are those theologians who are of the view that demons can indwell the bodies of both unbelievers and Christians. It is believed that this dichotomy may continue for a very long time to come as the debate rages on.

Demonization occurs when a fallen angel, now a demon, enters and occupies the body of an unbeliever. I believe that demons cannot enter the bodies of Christian believers because the Christian's body is the temple of the Holy Spirit.

Theologians who assert that Christians can have demons in them are those who are in the healing and deliverance ministry. These theologians assert that Christians can have demons in them because of the manifestations they observe in these believers during prayer sessions.

The Assemblies of God does not accept the premise that Christians can be inhabited by demons.[1]

In my opinion, answering the question as to whether a Christian can have a demon may be difficult without first taking a closer look at the following questions:

1. Who is a Christian?
2. Are all the people we see in the church and places of Christian worship Christians?

John 3:3 states: "Jesus answered and said to him 'Most assuredly, I say to you, unless one is born again, he cannot see the kingdom of God.'" Romans 10:9-10 says "if you confess with your mouth the Lord Jesus and believe in your heart that God has raised him from the dead, you will be saved. For with the heart one believes to righteousness, and with the mouth confession is made to salvation."

In accordance with the Scriptures quoted in the previous paragraph, when someone is led through the salvation process to confess Jesus Christ as Lord and Savior, we all assume that the person is born again and is saved; but is he truly saved? I believe it is only God who knows those who are genuinely saved and those who are not. For Jesus said, "not everyone who says to me, 'Lord, Lord,' shall enter the kingdom of heaven, but he who does the will of my Father in heaven" (Matthew 7:21). The import of this statement is that there may be a number of people who seat in the pews of churches every Sunday but probably are not Christians per se. When such people, who are part of the congregation and come to church regularly, manifest demons during prayer sessions, the natural reaction is that Christians can have demons indwelling them.

The Lord Jesus also warned us in Matthew 7:22-23 "Many will say to me in that day, 'Lord, Lord, have we not prophesied in your name, cast out demons in your name, and done many wonders in your name?' And then I will declare to them, 'I never knew you; depart from me, you who practice lawlessness!'" Until we are one hundred per cent sure that someone is a Christian (but it is only God who knows), the assertion that a Christian can have a demon indwelling his body may be in serious error.

The Issue of *Free Will* of Man

As to whether Christians can have demons dwelling in their bodies, it may also be pertinent to look at the issue of the *free will* of humans. Because of the *free will* that God has given to humans and angels; everyone is free to submit to whomsoever he desires. Someone may be a Christian, but if he decides to obey the Devil and live in sin, he becomes the devil's slave. Consequently, a demon has every right to interfere in the life of such a Christian who has decided to live in sin in obedience to the Devil. Romans 6:16 states: "Do you not know that to whom you present yourselves to obey, you are that one's slaves whom you obey, whether of sin to death or of obedience to righteousness?" I am of the view that a Christian who is filled with the Holy Spirit and being led by the Spirit of God (Romans 8:14) cannot be indwelt by any demon. In fact such a Christian is a great deterrent to the Devil and demons. Hence the Scriptures command Christians to be filled with the Holy Spirit (Ephesians 5:18).

Demonization and Demonic Interference

Demonization and **Demonic Interference** are two different stages of demonic activity in the lives of humans. Demons can seriously interfere in the life of a Christian and create all kinds of problems for the victim but they cannot inhabit his body. While demons seriously interfere in the life of a Christian, that believer may manifest demonic presence when the power of the Holy Spirit is present. This does not mean that the demon is dwelling inside the body of that believer. When a demon enters a human body, the person is said to be demonized because the demon has virtually taken a foothold in that human body; and I believe this can only happen with unbelievers.

An excellent example is the Gadarene demoniac who was at times controlled and driven by the demons (Mark 5:1-17). My point here is that the fact that a Christian manifests a demonic presence during a healing and deliverance session does not necessarily imply the believer has the demon dwelling in his body. That Christian is most probably being oppressed by the demon from outside of the victim's body—in other words, the demon is seriously interfering in his life. This Christian may be living in sin resulting in this demonic interference. Demonic interference or oppression may also occur as a result of a generational curse.

Someone may ask how these demons are sometimes able to speak through these Christians during healing and deliverance prayer meetings if the demons are not dwelling in the bodies of their victims. While a demon is seriously interfering in the life of a Christian, the former is sometimes able to temporarily take control of the vocal organs of the latter to speak. I wish to emphasize here again that Christians who live in holiness and obedience to Jesus Christ are a deterrent to demons; and there is no room for these demons in a believer's body.

The deeper a Christian lives in sin, the wider the door for demons to interfere in the life of that Christian. This trend may go on to the extreme in which case the demons may take over their victims completely. The degree to which demons interfere in the life of a Christian is dependent entirely on how close or how far that believer is to the Lord Jesus. "The name of the Lord is a strong tower; the righteous run to it and are safe"(Proverbs 18:10). My view is that a Christian living in holiness in the light of Scripture, under the grace of God in the power of the Holy Spirit, cannot be indwelt by any demon. However, demons have the capability to oppress or interfere in the life of Christians if they are given the opportunity.

Demons can Interfere in the Normal Functioning of the Human body

Demons can interfere in the normal functioning of the human body. There is the story of the woman with the "issue of blood" for twelve years. Physicians could not heal her until she met Jesus (Mark 5:25-34). In this particular case, we cannot tell exactly what went wrong with the woman's body system. One thing we know is that the woman's body was not functioning as God created it. Something was definitely wrong with her menstrual cycle until she met Jesus. I am of the view that a demon was seriously interfering in the regular menstrual cycle of this woman; and that was why the flow of the blood would not stop.

A Young Woman Healed of an *Issue of blood*

About four years ago a young woman in her early twenties started to visit us in church. About the fourth Sunday when we closed the regular morning service, I was surprised this young lady followed me to my office. I asked her if I could help her. She said she needed some anointing oil to use at home. That surprised me so I asked "for what?" At first she was reluctant to speak but as I insisted, she opened up and said: "I will tell you but please don't tell anybody." I told her I keep confidential matters of my members as CONFIDENTIAL.

It was an "Issue of Blood"

The lady went on to tell me that for almost two years she has been bleeding continuously non-stop; twenty four hours a day, seven days a week. She has seen all the medical specialists in the Washington Metro area. The medical specialists have prescribed all kinds of medications but her condition has remained the same. She also intimated that the medical specialists even administered some special medication injections which they claimed would have stopped the flow of the blood immediately, but it did not work. She said after that last effort the physicians gave up on her.

I told her that if that was her problem, it was not anointing oil per se that would bring her healing. I had a short talk with her and explained that her "issue of blood" problem was probably due to a demonic cause. She then agreed with me for prayer. I laid my hand on her, prayed and rebuked the demon causing the flow of blood for almost two years. I told her that in the name of Jesus Christ she was healed and that she should believe that she had been healed. She then said goodbye and left my office.

Very early in the morning the following day, the young woman called me. She said "Pastor, when I came home yesterday I checked to see if the blood has stopped flowing but unfortunately it was still flowing. When I was going to bed I checked again and it was still flowing. I went to bed and woke up at about 3:00am to use the bathroom and to my pleasant surprise the blood has ceased flowing. Pastor, for the excitement and joy that filled my heart, I could not sleep again and just waiting till this morning to inform you." We praised the Lord as I rejoiced with her for the fact that Jesus is truly merciful and a healer indeed.

Two weeks later she came to give a testimony in church. This time there was no mention of CONFIDENTIALITY. The young woman narrated everything in detail to the glory of the living God. The sickness that medical science and pharmacology could not help because a demon was the cause, this woman received her healing in the name of Jesus Christ. Praise God! We give all the glory to Jesus Christ who delegated his authority to believers to destroy every work of the Devil in His name. Halleluia! Ladies and Gentlemen, if your sickness, disease or pain would not yield to medical science and pharmacology, do not remain there suffering. Seek the help of any pastor in the healing and deliverance ministry of Jesus Christ. For Christ has already paid the price for your salvation, healing and deliverance from demonic hold on the cross at Calvary.

MEDICAL SCIENCE, PHARMACOLOGY AND MEDICAL DOCTORS

I wish to state categorically clear here that I have great respect for our medical doctors and all the paramedical staff for the wonderful work they perform to save human lives daily. All I am saying in this book is that when a particular sickness, disease or pain in the human body goes beyond the wisdom and medical knowledge of our hospitals; a demon may probably be the cause and their patients should seek help from an anointed Pastor of God in the healing and deliverance ministry where Jesus Christ is Lord and Savior. God bless all of you.

CHAPTER SIXTEEN

Spiritual Marriage

What is a "spiritual marriage?" A spiritual marriage is contracted when a demon through a human agent marries another human being in the spirit realm. The consequences of such a marriage are numerous and more often than not, the victim may not even be aware for a long time. This is a spiritual problem that is common knowledge among many African pastors, especially those from West Africa.

At my healing and deliverance meetings, I have often heard demons spoke clearly, using the vocal organs of their victims, to claim that the victims were their spouses. The victims may be males or females. This is a situation where the demon exercises full control in the spirit realm. These spiritual marriages most of the time, are contracted through very close family members (parents, children, siblings, etc.).

The following are some of the unfortunate consequences of such a marriage:

Marriage. When someone is in a spiritual marriage, the demon may prevent the victim from marrying anyone in the physical realm. The demons do this by scaring all suitors away. I have seen ladies and gentlemen come to church in their thirties and early forties who were still not married. A brief chat with most of them reveals that gentlemen come to date these ladies and vice versa but such relationships do not go beyond six months when they come to an abrupt end. You ask for the reasons why these relationships come to an abrupt end, and most of these men and women say their suitors just walk out of their lives without giving them any reasons.

A Gentleman Who Could Not Marry

There was this gentleman, Kofi (not the real name) in his early forties who could not marry simply because he said something keeps him away from females. Kofi was in a very good employment and though he wanted to marry, he just could not do so for an unknown reason. He came to my deliverance service and after hearing his story, I explained to him that he was probably in a spiritual marriage. I took him through the initial process in order to break the spiritual marriage. When I started praying for Kofi, he manifested strangely and fell on the floor. I prayed to nullify and break the spiritual marriage and commanded the spirit to leave in the name of Jesus. The demon violently threw him down again and left. He remained on the floor for some time before getting back on his feet. Kofi testified immediately that something had come out of him and he felt very 'light' and free. I knew the spiritual marriage was broken. He is now married and enjoying a great marital home.

Demon Interference with Pregnancy

Pregnancy. The second situation is that the demon may allow the person in a spiritual marriage to marry in the physical realm but the woman will never be pregnant. There was this lady, Amina (not her real name), who was invited to church by her friend. Amina was married for ten years but has never been pregnant. According to her, the husband has decided that their marriage was to end within three months when the lease on their apartment expires. During prayer time, Amina manifested, shook violently and fell to the floor. I asked that she should be brought to the front where I prayed for her, broke that spiritual marriage in the name of Jesus Christ and commanded the spirit to leave. The following month Amina came back to inform me that she was pregnant for the first time in ten years! She delivered a baby boy to the glory of God and has even had her second baby already.

Successive Miscarriages
May be a Sign of a Spiritual Marriage

Miscarriages. The third situation is that a woman in a spiritual marriage may marry in the physical realm and even be pregnant but within the first three or four months of the pregnancy, the woman will have a dream in which someone comes to have sex with her. When this occurs, the woman will have a miscarriage of the pregnancy within 24 hours. This will be the pattern throughout the woman's life if the spiritual marriage is not broken. It is one of the most frustrating situations that any married couple can face. The truth is that until the spiritual marriage is broken, this trend may continue for a long time.

A woman who was brought to church in Ghana had suffered three consecutive miscarriages. I explained to her that she was probably in a spiritual marriage and that could be the cause; she was very surprised and could not believe me. I asked her to renounce the spiritual marriage and to say that she did not want it again. She did and I prayed for her deliverance as I nullified the spiritual marriage. The next pregnancy stabilized and she delivered her child. We give all the glory to Jesus Christ who has delegated authority to believers to destroy the works of the devil.

Demons have the Capability to Interfere in a Marriage

Demonic Interference. A fourth situation is that a demon spirit in a spiritual marriage may stand between husband and wife in the physical realm to interfere in their marriage. The demon sometimes creates misunderstanding and confusion in the marriage in such a way that almost every conversation will end up in a quarrel. The aim of the demon is to break the marriage through divorce. Many marriages end up in divorce simply because one spouse may be involved in a spiritual marriage. When a marriage counselor is unable to help, the couple must seek spiritual deliverance from a pastor in the healing and deliverance ministry.

Breaking a Spiritual Marriage

How do we break a spiritual marriage? First, the victim must know that he or she is in a spiritual marriage. The individual must confess that he or she does not want the marriage any longer. This confession denies the demon any rights to remain in that spiritual marriage. The victim must also confess any known sins associated with that spiritual marriage and ask for forgiveness. If the spiritual marriage came out of a covenant with a demonic shrine, then that covenant must be rejected and nullified with the blood of Jesus and broken.

Then, pleading the blood of Jesus Christ, a prayer of deliverance to nullify and break that marriage must be offered and the demon involved must be commanded to leave in Jesus' name. Any Christian, living in holiness, should be able to break a spiritual marriage but where there is no breakthrough, the victim must seek the help of an anointed servant of God who is in the healing and deliverance ministry. Some spiritual marriages may be broken instantly while in other cases it may take a little while.

One Sunday afternoon during a deliverance service, I was praying for a young woman in church when she manifested a demon spirit. By the leading of the Holy Spirit, I knew that the lady was in a spiritual marriage. I led her through the process to break a spiritual marriage. As I continued to pray to break that spiritual marriage, the demon spoke out loud me. I asked her to renounce the spiritual marriage and to say that she did not want it again. She did and I prayed for her deliverance as I nullified the spiritual marriage. The next pregnancy stabilized and she delivered her child. We give all the glory to Jesus Christ who has delegated authority to believers to destroy the works of the devil.

Demons have the Capability to Interfere in a Marriage

Demonic Interference. A fourth situation is that a demon spirit in a spiritual marriage may stand between husband and wife in the physical realm to interfere in their marriage. The demon sometimes creates misunderstanding and confusion in the marriage in such a way that almost every conversation will end up in a quarrel. The aim of the demon is to break the marriage through divorce. Many marriages end up in divorce simply because one spouse may be involved in a spiritual marriage. When a marriage counselor is unable to help, the couple must seek spiritual deliverance from a pastor in the healing and deliverance ministry.

Breaking a Spiritual Marriage

How do we break a spiritual marriage? First, the victim must know that he or she is in a spiritual marriage. The individual must confess that he or she does not want the marriage any longer. This confession denies the demon any rights to remain in that spiritual marriage. The victim must also confess any known sins associated with that spiritual marriage and ask for forgiveness. If the spiritual marriage came out of a covenant with a demonic shrine, then that covenant must be rejected and nullified with the blood of Jesus and broken.

Then, pleading the blood of Jesus Christ, a prayer of deliverance to nullify and break that marriage must be offered and the demon involved must be commanded to leave in Jesus' name. Any Christian, living in holiness, should be able to break a spiritual marriage but where there is no breakthrough, the victim must seek the help of an anointed servant of God who is in the healing and deliverance ministry. Some spiritual marriages may be broken instantly while in other cases it may take a little while.

One Sunday afternoon during a deliverance service, I was praying for a young woman in church when she manifested a demon spirit. By the leading of the Holy Spirit, I knew that the lady was in a spiritual marriage. I led her through the process to break a spiritual marriage. As I continued to pray to break that spiritual marriage, the demon spoke out loud using the vocal organs of the victim. The lady shouted: "I divorce her." I knew straight away that it was the demon speaking. She repeated this statement (I divorce her) two or three times, fell to the floor and started saying, "thank you Jesus," "thank you Jesus." I also said "thank you Jesus" because I knew that her spiritual marriage was broken and that she was free from her bondage.

CHAPTER SEVENTEEN

Covenants/Agreements with the Devil and Demonic Shrines/Altars

What is a covenant or an agreement with the Devil? It is usually a verbal agreement with the Devil which may be sealed with the blood of an animal at a demonic altar. Why such a covenant? Humans go into such covenants when they go to seek protection or some favor from the Devil for themselves and/or their entire families. When the covenant is sealed, the Devil then cunningly takes authority over the human victim or family according to the terms of the covenant or agreement.

In reality, in such agreements, the human being has submitted himself under the authority of the Devil. Usually, enshrined in such a covenant are dos' and don'ts for the human victim. From time immemorial, the Devil knows that man has never been very successful with rules of dos' and don'ts. Therefore, the Devil knows that it would be a matter of time when the victim will contravene one of the terms or rules of the covenant. When that happens, the Devil begins to exact his pound of flesh on that victim and his family according to the terms of the covenant.

The Consequences of Breaking the Terms of a Satanic Covenant

Sometimes, someone in the family may fall sick seriously; while at other times a family member may suddenly die. Then it dawns on them to go back to the shrine to find out the cause of the sickness or the sudden death. This is the time the Devil will tell them the violations that caused the sickness or death. The Devil will then ask for so many things (a ram, a cow, a chicken and some alcoholic drinks, etc.) to be brought to the shrine for pacification rituals. Ladies and gentlemen, the devil can never be pacified with anything and he has nothing good to offer you. He is still the same old Lucifer with many tricks; he came to steal, to kill and to destroy humanity (John 10:10). Keep away from him and seek true life and peace in Jesus Christ.

Generational Curses and Covenants

Generational curses are curses upon a particular person or family which may affect other generations after them. Covenants with the Devil may also be binding on successive generations in a family depending on the terms of the covenant. Within the past twelve years as a pastor, I have interacted with some pastors in this nation who do not believe in ancestral and generational curses. Apart from the Devil deceiving humanity into sin through Adam and Eve, such pastors do not believe that the Devil has anything to do with the problems of humanity. The belief of such pastors is rather unfortunate because that is the grand strategy of the Devil to make humanity exonerate him (Devil) totally from our problems on this earth. The Devil is happy when we blame each other and leave him out. I am not saying that all our problems per se should be blamed on the Devil, but he has a hand in most of them.

Consequences of Generational Curses and Demonic Covenants

I was born in Ghana in West Africa and grew up in that culture. I have seen and lived with families that suffer one tragedy after another but nobody understands. I know of families in which insanity has been traced to three or four generations before them. Everybody in the town or village knows—it is an open secret. Sometimes, in every generation, may be one or two people are insane in that family.

I am not writing about people who live in the big cities where nobody can trace their families. I am referring to the typical village or town set up where everybody knows everybody in every home and family, at least in Africa. I know of families in which some of their pregnant women go to deliver and the mothers die while the babies survive or babies die at birth. These fatalities have been known to occur from one generation to another in such families.

A Repetitive Fatality in a Family may be an Indication of an Ancestral or Generational Curse

There are also families in which someone dies by drowning in the sea or in a river in every generation. You may also be surprised to know that there are families in which the men do not live beyond fifty years. I knew a gentleman a few years back who was about to turn forty years. He intimated that he had been gripped by fear because in his family some of the men suddenly die between forty and forty-five years old. Many people may not understand, but the real reason may be rooted in an ancestral curse or covenant. I told this gentleman: "You are a Christian and all we need to do is to break the covenant or ancestral curse that may be over your life." Indeed, we fasted, prayed and broke that curse over his life in Jesus' name. The gentleman is still alive and almost fifty years old now.

There was this military officer in Ghana who died in a vehicle accident in the early 1980's. It was at the funeral that we learnt that in their family, many of the men die before they celebrate their fiftieth birthday. I know of families in which their women never stay in their marital homes beyond five years. These women marry, but their husbands divorce them before the marriage is five years old. These divorces may have spiritual causes which may be deep-seated in ancestral curses. Most of these women go back to their parental homes (that is the African culture) with one or two children following them.

Intelligent Men who won't Work any Job

There are also families in which the men are very intelligent. These men get the highest academic awards through college education but strangely, when they graduate they never want to work any job. These fine brains just stay home as the spirit of laziness takes control of their lives. Someone may wonder how these sad occurrences happen? These rather sad occurrences are the consequences of ancestral curses and covenants with the Devil and demonic altars. Interestingly, the "suffering generation" has no clue as to how those demonic covenants were contracted with the Devil by the generations before them. I can only assure you that as Christians we have authority to nullify and break those covenants and destroy any ancestral curses that may be upon us.

We have also seen families in which everyone is very hard working, yet they live in abject poverty from one generation to the other. What is the problem and what do they do with the salaries they earn? They have no explanations to their woes. It is either a generational curse or a covenant with a demonic shrine that has been violated and the Devil is executing his portion of the covenant. One important fact is the repetitive nature of these sad occurrences and that is what makes it a generational curse.

Seek Help as Quickly as Possible

When we understand the causes of such problems then we can seek help. Christians in such families may need prayer to break any curses over their lives and to nullify and cancel any ancestral covenants that may be affecting them. After all, the blood of Jesus Christ has fully paid for everything on our behalf. Therefore, if you observe any such recurring trends in your family line which may be affecting your life, you need to seek help quickly from your pastor. If your pastor is unable to help, you may seek help from another servant of God who is in the healing and deliverance ministry. Remember, Jesus Christ came to set the captives free.

So what have I Been Trying to Convey to You?

Throughout the pages of this book, I have been trying to explain to you that there are certain sicknesses which Medical science and pharmacology have neither clues nor cures. Such sicknesses are caused by demons. Therefore if your sickness falls into that category and the medical specialists are unable to help you, do not sit there and continue to suffer. Ladies and gentlemen, arise and go seek help from any pastor in the healing and deliverance ministry. If you live in the state of Maryland, please visit us on a Sunday morning worship service or in the afternoon healing and deliverance service; in the name of Jesus Christ we will help and pray with you.

OUR IMMUTABLE CONFESSION

We boldly confess that Jesus Christ Is the Son of God. He came in the flesh to die for our sins on the cross at Calvary. He was buried and the third day He arose from the dead. He ascended into heaven and seated on the right hand of God the Father. He is our Lord, our Savior, our Master, our Friend, our Healer, our Deliverer, our Rock and our Salvation.

May the Lord Jesus Christ help you to understand this confession and be able to accept Him as your Lord and your Savior.

I hope this book has been helpful to you in one way or the other. If it has been helpful then recommend it to a friend. Thank you and God bless you.

NOTES

Introduction

1. Encyclopedia.thefreedictionary.com/illness [accessed January 19, 2008]
2. World Council of Churches. *Healing and Wholeness: The Churches' Role in Health. The Report of a Study by the World Council of Churches* (Geneva, Switzerland: World Council of Churches, 1990), 6.
3. http://encyclopedia.thefreedictionary.com/illness [accessed January 19, 2008]
4. Encyclopedia.freedictionary.com/illness [accessed January 19, 2008]
5. Random House Webster's College Dictionary (New York, NY: Random House Inc., 1996), 1244.
6. Ibid., 384.
7. Ibid., 670.

8. Medical-dictionary.thefreedictionary.com/illness [accessed January 19, 2008].

Chapter Two

1. Origen, *The Fundamental Doctrines,* in W.A. Jurgens, ed., *The Faith of the Early Fathers* (Collegeville: The Liturgical Press, 1970), 192.
2. Lester Sumrall, *Demons: The Answer Book* (New Kensington, PA: Whitaker House, 2003), 37.
3. United Church of God, *Is There Really a Devil* (U.S.A.: United Church of God, an International Association, 2001), 21.
4. Charles H. Kraft, *Defeating Dark Angels,* Breaking Demonic Oppression in the Believer's Life (Ventura, CA: Regal Books, 1992), 19.

Chapter Four

1. George A. Birch, *The Deliverance Ministry* (Cathedral City, CA: Horizon House Publishers, 1998), 35.
2. Steve Gallagher, *At the Altar of Sexual Idolatry* (Dry Ridge, KY: Pure Life Ministries, 2000), 170.

NOTES

Introduction

1. Encyclopedia.thefreedictionary.com/illness [accessed January 19, 2008]
2. World Council of Churches. *Healing and Wholeness: The Churches' Role in Health. The Report of a Study by the World Council of Churches* (Geneva, Switzerland: World Council of Churches, 1990), 6.
3. http://encyclopedia.thefreedictionary.com/illness [accessed January 19, 2008]
4. Encyclopedia.freedictionary.com/illness [accessed January 19, 2008]
5. Random House Webster's College Dictionary (New York, NY: Random House Inc., 1996), 1244.
6. Ibid., 384.
7. Ibid., 670.

8. Medical-dictionary.thefreedictionary.com/illness [accessed January 19, 2008].

Chapter Two

1. Origen, *The Fundamental Doctrines,* in W.A. Jurgens, ed., *The Faith of the Early Fathers* (Collegeville: The Liturgical Press, 1970), 192.
2. Lester Sumrall, *Demons: The Answer Book* (New Kensington, PA: Whitaker House, 2003), 37.
3. United Church of God, *Is There Really a Devil* (U.S.A.: United Church of God, an International Association, 2001), 21.
4. Charles H. Kraft, *Defeating Dark Angels,* Breaking Demonic Oppression in the Believer's Life (Ventura, CA: Regal Books, 1992), 19.

Chapter Four

1. George A. Birch, *The Deliverance Ministry* (Cathedral City, CA: Horizon House Publishers, 1998), 35.
2. Steve Gallagher, *At the Altar of Sexual Idolatry* (Dry Ridge, KY: Pure Life Ministries, 2000), 170.

Chapter Seven

1. John M. Last, "Filth Diseases," The Gale Group Inc., Macmillan Reference (New York, USA: *Gale Encyclopedia of Public Health,* 2002.

Chapter Eleven

1. Encyclopedia.freedictionary.com/illness [accessed January 18, 2008].
2. Ibid.
3. Diane Dew, Is Mental Illness caused by Sin or a Demon? http://www.dianedew.com/qa-mental.htm [accessed January 18, 2008].
4. George A. Birch, *The Deliverance Ministry* (Cathedral City, CA: Horizon House Publishers, 1998), 80-81.

Chapter Twelve

1. K. Dua-Agyeman, *Covenant, Curses and Cure* (Kumasi, Ghana: Payless Printing Press, 1994), 5.

Chapter Thirteen

1. William F. Arndt and F. Wilbur Gingrich, *Greek-English Lexicon of the New Testament* (Chicago, IL: University of Chicago Press, 1952), 168.

Chapter Fifteen

1. The Assemblies of God, *Position Paper*, "Can Born-Again Believers Be Demon-possessed? (Springfield, MO: Gospel Publishing House, 1972).

CPSIA information can be obtained
at www.ICGtesting.com
Printed in the USA
FFOW02n0948150416
23293FF